Copyright © 2023 by Herman Strange (Author)

All rights reserved. This book or any portion thereof may not be reproduced or used in any manner whatsoever without the express written permission of the publisher except for the use of brief quotations in a book review.

This book is copyright protected. This is only for personal use. You cannot amend, distributor, sell, use, quote or paraphrase any part or the content within this book without the consent of the author. Please note the information contained within this document is for educational and entertainment purposes only. Every attempt has been made to provide accurate, up to date and reliable complete information. No warranties of any kind are expressed or implied.

Readers acknowledge that the author is not engaging in the rendering of legal, financial, medical or professional advice. The content of this book has been derived from various sources. Please consult a licensed professional before attempting any techniques outlined in this book.

By reading this document, the readers agree that under no circumstances are the author responsible for any losses, direct or indirect, which are incurred as a result of the use of information contained within this document, including but not limited to errors, omissions or inaccuracies.

Thank you very much for reading this book.

Title: Machine Learning and AI in Clinical Practice
Subtitle: Revolutionizing Diagnosis and Treatment Strategies

Series: Rise of Cognitive Computing: AI Evolution from Origins to Adoption
Author: Herman Strange

Table of Contents

Introduction 6
    Definition of AI and its applications in healthcare 6
    The purpose of the book 8
    Brief overview of the chapters 11

Chapter 1: The History of AI in Medicine 14
    Early AI applications in healthcare 14
    Key milestones in AI development in medicine 16
    Successes and challenges of AI in medicine 19
    Current state of AI in healthcare 21

Chapter 2: Machine Learning Fundamentals 24
    Basics of machine learning algorithms 24
    Types of machine learning in healthcare 27
    Data preparation and feature engineering 29
    Model selection and evaluation 32

Chapter 3: Machine Learning Applications in Diagnosis 35
    Use of machine learning in diagnostic imaging 35
    Machine learning in pathology and dermatology 39
    Applications in predicting and diagnosing disease 41
    Challenges and limitations of machine learning in diagnosis 44

Chapter 4: Machine Learning Applications in Treatment 46

Personalized medicine and precision oncology............... 46

Machine learning in drug discovery and development ..50

Predicting treatment outcomes with machine learning .54

Challenges and limitations of machine learning in treatment.. 57

Chapter 5: Machine Learning Applications in Healthcare Operations **61**

Healthcare data management and analysis 61

Streamlining clinical workflows with machine learning 65

Predictive maintenance in medical equipment 68

Challenges and limitations of machine learning in healthcare operations 73

Chapter 6: The Future of AI in Medicine **76**

Current and potential future AI applications in medicine 76

The role of AI in transforming healthcare 79

Ethical and social considerations in AI in medicine 82

Opportunities and challenges in future AI development in medicine 86

Conclusion **89**

The potential of AI in transforming healthcare 89

The need for continued research and development in AI in medicine 92

The importance of ethical and responsible AI development and use in healthcare *94*
Final thoughts and recommendations for further reading *97*
Glossary **100**
Potential References.. **103**

Introduction

Definition of AI and its applications in healthcare

Artificial Intelligence (AI) is a rapidly growing field that aims to create machines that can perform tasks that typically require human intelligence, such as learning, problem-solving, and decision-making. AI is often categorized into two types: narrow or weak AI, which is designed to perform specific tasks, and general or strong AI, which has the ability to reason, plan, and solve problems across different domains. While we are still far from achieving general AI, narrow AI is already being used in many industries, including healthcare.

In healthcare, AI has the potential to revolutionize how we diagnose and treat diseases, manage healthcare operations, and improve patient outcomes. Some of the key applications of AI in healthcare include:

- Medical imaging: AI algorithms can analyze medical images, such as X-rays and MRIs, to help diagnose diseases and detect abnormalities.

- Clinical decision-making: AI can help healthcare providers make more accurate diagnoses and treatment plans by analyzing patient data and providing recommendations based on best practices.

- Drug discovery: AI can be used to identify new drug targets, predict drug efficacy and toxicity, and optimize drug development processes.

- Healthcare operations: AI can help streamline clinical workflows, optimize resource allocation, and reduce costs by analyzing data from electronic health records (EHRs) and other sources.

While the potential benefits of AI in healthcare are significant, there are also some challenges and limitations to consider. For example, AI algorithms may be biased or lack transparency, which could lead to incorrect diagnoses or treatments. Additionally, AI may not be able to fully replace the human element in healthcare, such as the importance of empathy and communication between patients and providers.

In this book, we will explore the history of AI in medicine, the fundamentals of machine learning algorithms, and the key applications of AI in diagnosis, treatment, and healthcare operations. We will also discuss the challenges and limitations of AI in healthcare and the potential future developments in this field. By the end of this book, readers will have a comprehensive understanding of how AI is transforming healthcare and the opportunities and challenges that lie ahead.

The purpose of the book

The purpose of this book is to provide a comprehensive overview of the applications of machine learning and AI in clinical practice, and to explore how these technologies are revolutionizing diagnosis and treatment strategies in healthcare. The book is intended for a broad audience, including healthcare providers, researchers, policy makers, and anyone interested in understanding the potential of AI in healthcare.

Specifically, the book aims to:

1. Provide a historical overview of AI in medicine: In Chapter 1, we will explore the early applications of AI in healthcare and the key milestones that have led to the current state of AI in medicine. This historical context will help readers understand the evolution of the field and the challenges that have been overcome.

2. Explain the fundamentals of machine learning: In Chapter 2, we will provide an introduction to the basics of machine learning algorithms, including the different types of algorithms used in healthcare and the process of data preparation and model selection. This chapter will be useful for readers who are not familiar with machine learning but want to understand how it works.

3. Explore the applications of machine learning in diagnosis: In Chapter 3, we will focus on the use of machine learning in diagnostic imaging, pathology, dermatology, and disease prediction. We will examine the successes and challenges of machine learning in diagnosis, and highlight the potential benefits of these technologies for patients and healthcare providers.

4. Investigate the applications of machine learning in treatment: In Chapter 4, we will discuss how machine learning is being used in personalized medicine, precision oncology, drug discovery, and treatment outcome prediction. We will explore the potential of these technologies to improve patient outcomes and reduce healthcare costs.

5. Analyze the applications of machine learning in healthcare operations: In Chapter 5, we will examine how machine learning is being used to manage healthcare data, streamline clinical workflows, and predict equipment maintenance needs. We will also discuss the challenges and limitations of these technologies in healthcare operations.

6. Discuss the future of AI in medicine: In Chapter 6, we will explore the potential future applications of AI in medicine, the role of AI in transforming healthcare, and the ethical and social considerations that must be taken into account as AI becomes more widespread in healthcare.

By the end of this book, readers will have a comprehensive understanding of the potential of machine learning and AI in healthcare, as well as the challenges and limitations that must be overcome to fully realize that potential. We hope that this book will serve as a valuable resource for anyone interested in the intersection of AI and medicine, and inspire further research and development in this exciting field.

Brief overview of the chapters

This book is divided into six chapters, each of which focuses on a different aspect of machine learning and AI in clinical practice. Here is a brief overview of what you can expect from each chapter:

Chapter 1: The History of AI in Medicine In this chapter, we will explore the early applications of AI in healthcare and the key milestones that have led to the current state of AI in medicine. We will examine the successes and challenges of AI in medicine, and provide historical context for readers to better understand the evolution of the field.

Chapter 2: Machine Learning Fundamentals In this chapter, we will provide an introduction to the basics of machine learning algorithms, including the different types of algorithms used in healthcare and the process of data preparation and model selection. We will explain the key concepts of machine learning and provide examples of how these concepts are applied in clinical practice.

Chapter 3: Machine Learning Applications in Diagnosis In this chapter, we will explore the use of machine learning in diagnostic imaging, pathology, dermatology, and disease prediction. We will examine the successes and challenges of machine learning in diagnosis, and highlight the potential benefits of these technologies for patients and healthcare providers.

Chapter 4: Machine Learning Applications in Treatment In this chapter, we will discuss how machine learning is being used in personalized medicine, precision oncology, drug discovery, and treatment outcome prediction. We will explore the potential of these technologies to improve patient outcomes and reduce healthcare costs.

Chapter 5: Machine Learning Applications in Healthcare Operations In this chapter, we will examine how machine learning is being used to manage healthcare data, streamline clinical workflows, and predict equipment maintenance needs. We will also discuss the challenges and limitations of these technologies in healthcare operations.

Chapter 6: The Future of AI in Medicine In this chapter, we will explore the potential future applications of AI in medicine, the role of AI in transforming healthcare, and the ethical and social considerations that must be taken into account as AI becomes more widespread in healthcare. We will also examine the opportunities and challenges of future AI development in medicine.

By the end of this book, readers will have a comprehensive understanding of the potential of machine learning and AI in healthcare, as well as the challenges and limitations that must be overcome to fully realize that potential. Each chapter is designed to build on the previous one, providing readers with a deep and nuanced understanding of this exciting field.

Chapter 1: The History of AI in Medicine
Early AI applications in healthcare

Artificial intelligence has been used in healthcare for several decades, with early applications focused on decision support systems and rule-based expert systems. These early AI systems were designed to mimic the decision-making processes of human experts in various medical fields. Here are some examples of early AI applications in healthcare:

1. MYCIN - One of the earliest examples of an AI system in healthcare, MYCIN was developed in the early 1970s by researchers at Stanford University. MYCIN was a rule-based expert system designed to help diagnose and treat bacterial infections. The system was able to ask questions of the clinician, such as the patient's symptoms and medical history, and provide a recommendation for treatment based on its knowledge of infectious diseases.

2. Internist-I - Developed in the late 1970s by researchers at the University of Pittsburgh, Internist-I was a rule-based expert system designed to help diagnose complex medical cases. The system used a knowledge base of medical information to provide a list of possible diagnoses based on the patient's symptoms and medical history.

3. DENDRAL - Developed in the 1960s and 70s by researchers at Stanford University, DENDRAL was an early

example of an AI system designed for chemical analysis. The system was able to interpret mass spectrometry data and suggest the most likely chemical structure of an unknown molecule. While not directly related to healthcare, DENDRAL laid the foundation for many of the AI techniques used in medical applications today.

4. PUFF - Developed in the 1980s, PUFF was a rule-based expert system designed to help diagnose pulmonary diseases. The system was able to take in a patient's symptoms and medical history and suggest a list of possible diagnoses based on its knowledge of respiratory diseases.

These early AI applications in healthcare were limited in their capabilities and often required significant manual input from clinicians. However, they laid the foundation for future AI systems and demonstrated the potential for machine learning algorithms to improve medical diagnosis and treatment. As computing power increased and new AI techniques were developed, the field of AI in healthcare continued to evolve, leading to more advanced and sophisticated systems.

Key milestones in AI development in medicine

1. Deep Blue Defeats Chess Champion (1997) - While not directly related to healthcare, IBM's Deep Blue computer defeating world champion Garry Kasparov in a game of chess marked a significant milestone in the development of AI. The victory showcased the potential for AI to outperform human experts in complex tasks and inspired researchers in many fields to explore the capabilities of machine learning algorithms.

2. Diagnosis of Breast Cancer with Neural Networks (1994) - Researchers at the University of California, Los Angeles, developed a neural network algorithm that was able to accurately diagnose breast cancer based on mammogram images. The system demonstrated the potential for machine learning algorithms to improve the accuracy and speed of medical diagnosis.

3. Approval of Computer-Aided Diagnosis for Mammography (1998) - The U.S. Food and Drug Administration (FDA) approved the use of computer-aided diagnosis (CAD) for mammography, allowing radiologists to use machine learning algorithms to help detect breast cancer. This marked the first approval of an AI-based medical device by the FDA and opened the door for further AI applications in healthcare.

4. Watson Wins Jeopardy (2011) - IBM's Watson computer defeated human champions in the game show Jeopardy, showcasing the potential for natural language processing and machine learning algorithms to perform complex tasks. The victory also sparked interest in using AI to improve clinical decision-making.

5. AlphaGo Defeats Go Champion (2016) - Similar to Deep Blue's victory over Kasparov, Google's AlphaGo computer defeating world champion Lee Sedol in the game of Go demonstrated the potential for AI to outperform human experts in complex tasks with high levels of uncertainty.

6. Approval of AI-based Diagnostic Software (2018) - The FDA approved the first AI-based diagnostic software for the detection of diabetic retinopathy, a leading cause of blindness. The approval marked a significant milestone in the development of AI in healthcare and demonstrated the potential for machine learning algorithms to improve medical diagnosis and treatment.

These key milestones in AI development in medicine demonstrate the progress that has been made in the field of AI and the potential for machine learning algorithms to transform healthcare. As the field continues to evolve, we can expect to see more advanced and sophisticated AI systems that are able to improve the accuracy and speed of medical diagnosis, personalize treatment plans, and streamline healthcare operations.

Successes and challenges of AI in medicine

AI has shown promise in improving healthcare by enabling early detection, accurate diagnosis, personalized treatment, and better patient outcomes. Here are some examples of successes in AI in medicine:

1. Improved medical imaging: AI can analyze medical images such as X-rays, CT scans, and MRIs to identify patterns and anomalies that may be missed by human observers. For example, AI algorithms can detect early signs of lung cancer on CT scans, reducing the need for invasive biopsies and increasing the chances of successful treatment.

2. Predictive analytics: AI can be used to analyze large datasets of patient records to predict disease progression, identify high-risk patients, and personalize treatment plans. For example, AI algorithms can predict the likelihood of hospital readmission or adverse events in patients with chronic conditions, enabling proactive interventions to prevent complications.

3. Drug discovery and development: AI can accelerate the discovery of new drugs and reduce the time and cost of clinical trials. For example, AI algorithms can analyze large datasets of genetic and molecular data to identify potential drug targets and predict the safety and efficacy of new drugs.

However, there are also several challenges and limitations associated with the use of AI in medicine:

1. Data quality and bias: AI algorithms require large amounts of high-quality data to be trained effectively. However, healthcare data is often fragmented, incomplete, and biased, which can lead to inaccurate predictions and recommendations.

2. Interpretability and transparency: AI algorithms can be complex and difficult to interpret, making it challenging for healthcare providers to understand how they arrive at their recommendations. Lack of transparency can also make it difficult to identify and correct errors and biases in the algorithms.

3. Regulatory and ethical issues: The use of AI in medicine raises several ethical and regulatory concerns, including patient privacy, informed consent, and liability. There is also a risk of algorithmic bias, where AI systems may discriminate against certain patient populations or perpetuate existing healthcare disparities.

Overall, the successes of AI in medicine are promising, but it is essential to address the challenges and limitations to ensure that AI is used ethically and responsibly to improve patient outcomes.

Current state of AI in healthcare

The use of AI in healthcare has increased dramatically in recent years, driven by advances in machine learning algorithms, cloud computing, and big data analytics. AI has been deployed in a variety of healthcare settings, including hospitals, clinics, and research institutions. In this section, we will explore the current state of AI in healthcare and some of the key trends and challenges.

One of the key areas where AI is being used in healthcare is in medical imaging. Machine learning algorithms have been developed to analyze medical images and identify patterns and anomalies that may be difficult for human clinicians to detect. For example, in radiology, AI is being used to detect lung cancer, breast cancer, and other diseases at an early stage, improving patient outcomes.

Another area where AI is having a significant impact is in clinical decision support. By analyzing patient data, including electronic health records, laboratory results, and medical imaging, machine learning algorithms can help clinicians make more informed decisions about patient care. For example, AI can be used to identify patients who are at high risk of developing certain conditions, such as sepsis, and provide early warning signs to clinicians.

AI is also being used to develop new drugs and therapies. By analyzing large datasets of chemical and biological information, machine learning algorithms can help identify potential drug targets and predict the efficacy and safety of new drugs. This has the potential to significantly speed up the drug development process and bring new treatments to market more quickly.

Despite the many potential benefits of AI in healthcare, there are also significant challenges and concerns. One of the biggest challenges is the need for large amounts of high-quality data to train machine learning algorithms. In many cases, such data is not readily available, and efforts to collect and organize it can be time-consuming and costly.

Another challenge is the lack of transparency and interpretability of machine learning algorithms. Because these algorithms can learn complex patterns in data, it can be difficult to understand how they are making decisions. This can lead to concerns about bias, fairness, and the potential for errors or unintended consequences.

Finally, there are also concerns about the impact of AI on the roles and responsibilities of healthcare professionals. As machines become more capable of performing tasks traditionally done by humans, there is a risk that some jobs may be replaced or automated. At the same time, there is also the potential for new roles and opportunities to emerge, as clinicians work alongside machines to improve patient care.

Overall, the current state of AI in healthcare is one of rapid growth and development, with many exciting possibilities and significant challenges. As we move forward, it will be important to address these challenges and ensure that AI is used in a responsible and ethical manner to improve patient outcomes and advance medical knowledge.

Chapter 2: Machine Learning Fundamentals
Basics of machine learning algorithms

Machine learning algorithms are at the core of artificial intelligence and are used extensively in healthcare to analyze complex medical data and make accurate predictions. Machine learning is a subset of artificial intelligence that uses statistical techniques to enable machines to learn from data, identify patterns, and make decisions without being explicitly programmed.

At a high level, machine learning algorithms can be categorized into three broad types: supervised learning, unsupervised learning, and reinforcement learning. Each type of algorithm has its own strengths and weaknesses, and healthcare professionals must choose the most appropriate algorithm for a given task.

Supervised learning algorithms learn from labeled data, where the data has already been categorized into specific classes. These algorithms use labeled training data to identify patterns and relationships between the input data and the output labels. Common examples of supervised learning algorithms in healthcare include logistic regression, decision trees, random forests, and support vector machines.

Unsupervised learning algorithms, on the other hand, are used when the data is not labeled, and the machine is tasked with identifying patterns and relationships within the data on its own. Clustering and association rule mining are examples of unsupervised learning algorithms that are commonly used in healthcare.

Reinforcement learning is a type of machine learning where the algorithm learns by interacting with the environment and receiving feedback in the form of rewards or punishments. This type of learning is similar to how humans learn from trial and error. Reinforcement learning is being increasingly used in healthcare to optimize treatment plans and improve patient outcomes.

In addition to these types of algorithms, there are several other concepts that are important to understand when discussing machine learning. For example, feature selection is the process of selecting the most relevant features or variables to include in the analysis. This is important to reduce the complexity of the model and prevent overfitting.

Regularization is another important concept in machine learning that helps prevent overfitting by adding a penalty term to the loss function. This penalty term discourages the model from learning complex patterns that may be present in the training data but are not representative of the underlying relationship between the features and the output.

In summary, understanding the basics of machine learning algorithms is crucial for healthcare professionals who want to use AI to improve patient outcomes. There are several different types of algorithms, each with its own strengths and weaknesses, and choosing the right algorithm for a given task is essential for achieving accurate results.

Types of machine learning in healthcare

Machine learning is a subfield of artificial intelligence (AI) that enables computer systems to automatically learn and improve from experience without being explicitly programmed. In healthcare, machine learning has proven to be a valuable tool for analyzing vast amounts of data and extracting insights that can aid in medical decision-making.

There are several types of machine learning algorithms that are commonly used in healthcare, each with its unique advantages and limitations. The three primary types of machine learning algorithms are supervised learning, unsupervised learning, and reinforcement learning.

Supervised learning is a type of machine learning algorithm that involves training a model on labeled data to predict an output variable based on one or more input variables. In healthcare, supervised learning algorithms are commonly used for tasks such as disease diagnosis and treatment prediction. For example, a supervised learning algorithm can be trained on a dataset of patient medical records and corresponding diagnoses to predict the diagnosis of a new patient based on their medical history.

Unsupervised learning is a type of machine learning algorithm that involves training a model on unlabeled data to uncover patterns and relationships in the data. In healthcare, unsupervised learning algorithms are commonly used for tasks such as patient clustering and anomaly detection. For example, an unsupervised learning algorithm can be trained on a dataset of patient medical records to group patients based on similar characteristics, such as demographics and medical history.

Reinforcement learning is a type of machine learning algorithm that involves training a model to make decisions in a dynamic environment based on a reward system. In healthcare, reinforcement learning algorithms are commonly used for tasks such as personalized treatment recommendation and clinical decision support. For example, a reinforcement learning algorithm can be trained to recommend personalized treatment plans for cancer patients based on their medical history and response to previous treatments.

Overall, machine learning is a powerful tool that has the potential to revolutionize healthcare by enabling more accurate diagnoses, personalized treatments, and streamlined clinical workflows. However, it is important to carefully consider the appropriate type of machine learning algorithm for each specific use case and to ensure that the data used to train these algorithms is representative and unbiased.

Data preparation and feature engineering

Data preparation and feature engineering are essential steps in the process of applying machine learning algorithms to healthcare data. This chapter will provide an overview of these steps and their importance in the success of machine learning models.

Importance of Data Preparation and Feature Engineering

Before applying machine learning algorithms to healthcare data, it is crucial to prepare the data and engineer features that are relevant to the task at hand. This involves several steps, including data cleaning, data normalization, feature selection, and feature extraction.

Data cleaning involves removing missing or corrupted data points and ensuring that the data is formatted consistently. Data normalization is the process of scaling data to ensure that it is within a consistent range, which can help prevent the model from being biased towards certain features. Feature selection involves identifying the most relevant features in the data that are likely to contribute to the model's accuracy. Feature extraction involves transforming raw data into features that are easier for the model to interpret.

The quality of the data and the features used in a machine learning model can significantly impact its accuracy and generalizability. Therefore, it is essential to carefully consider these steps during the development of a machine learning model.

Data Preparation Techniques

Data preparation involves several techniques that can be applied to healthcare data. These techniques include:

Data Cleaning

Data cleaning is an essential step in the data preparation process. It involves removing any missing or corrupted data points, ensuring that the data is formatted consistently, and handling outliers. Missing data can be handled using techniques such as mean imputation or regression imputation. Outliers can be detected using statistical techniques and removed or transformed to better fit the model.

Data Normalization

Data normalization is the process of scaling data to ensure that it is within a consistent range. This step is crucial for preventing the model from being biased towards certain features. Techniques for data normalization include min-max scaling and z-score normalization.

Feature Selection

Feature selection involves identifying the most relevant features in the data that are likely to contribute to the model's accuracy. This step is essential for reducing the dimensionality of the data, which can help prevent overfitting and improve the model's performance. Techniques for feature selection include correlation analysis, mutual information, and principal component analysis.

Feature Extraction

Feature extraction involves transforming raw data into features that are easier for the model to interpret. This step can help reduce the dimensionality of the data and improve the model's performance. Techniques for feature extraction include wavelet transforms, Fourier transforms, and time-series analysis.

Conclusion

Data preparation and feature engineering are critical steps in the development of machine learning models for healthcare data. These steps can significantly impact the accuracy and generalizability of the model, and therefore should be carefully considered during the model development process. Techniques such as data cleaning, data normalization, feature selection, and feature extraction can be applied to healthcare data to improve the quality of the data and the features used in the model.

Model selection and evaluation

Model selection and evaluation are critical steps in machine learning that help to ensure the accuracy and effectiveness of the models developed. In this section, we will discuss the different techniques and methods used for model selection and evaluation in healthcare.

Model Selection: The process of selecting a model involves choosing the best algorithm that can effectively solve a specific problem. In healthcare, this process is critical because the wrong model selection can result in incorrect diagnoses or inaccurate predictions. The following are some of the commonly used techniques for model selection:

1. Cross-validation: Cross-validation is a technique used to evaluate the performance of a model. This technique involves dividing the dataset into two parts: the training dataset and the validation dataset. The model is then trained on the training dataset and evaluated on the validation dataset. This process is repeated several times, and the average performance of the model is calculated.

2. Grid Search: Grid search is a technique used to find the best hyperparameters for a model. Hyperparameters are values that are set before the model is trained, and they can affect the model's performance. Grid search involves creating a grid of possible hyperparameters and training the model on

each combination of hyperparameters. The best-performing hyperparameters are then selected.

3. Random Search: Random search is similar to grid search, but it randomly selects hyperparameters rather than searching through a grid. This technique can be useful when there are a large number of hyperparameters to search through.

Model Evaluation: Once the model is selected, it is important to evaluate its performance to ensure that it is accurate and effective. The following are some commonly used techniques for model evaluation:

1. Confusion Matrix: A confusion matrix is a table that shows the number of true positives, true negatives, false positives, and false negatives for a model. It is used to evaluate the accuracy of a classification model.

2. Receiver Operating Characteristic (ROC) Curve: An ROC curve is a graph that shows the true positive rate (sensitivity) against the false positive rate (1-specificity) for different classification thresholds. It is used to evaluate the performance of a classification model.

3. Mean Absolute Error (MAE) and Mean Squared Error (MSE): MAE and MSE are metrics used to evaluate the performance of regression models. MAE measures the average absolute difference between the predicted and actual

values, while MSE measures the average squared difference between the predicted and actual values.

4. Cross-validation: Cross-validation can also be used to evaluate the performance of a model. By using different subsets of the dataset for training and validation, cross-validation can provide a more accurate estimate of the model's performance.

In conclusion, model selection and evaluation are critical steps in machine learning that ensure the accuracy and effectiveness of the models developed. Techniques such as cross-validation, grid search, and random search can be used for model selection, while confusion matrix, ROC curve, MAE, MSE, and cross-validation can be used for model evaluation. These techniques can be applied in healthcare to develop accurate and effective machine learning models.

Chapter 3: Machine Learning Applications in Diagnosis

Use of machine learning in diagnostic imaging

Medical imaging is one of the key areas where machine learning (ML) has shown great promise. It has the potential to significantly improve the accuracy and speed of diagnosis, reduce errors and variability, and enhance patient outcomes. In this section, we will discuss the use of machine learning in diagnostic imaging, including its current applications, challenges, and future possibilities.

1. Current Applications of ML in Diagnostic Imaging

Machine learning algorithms have been applied to various types of medical imaging, including radiography, computed tomography (CT), magnetic resonance imaging (MRI), and ultrasound. Some of the current applications of machine learning in diagnostic imaging are:

- Image segmentation: Machine learning algorithms can segment the medical images into various regions of interest, such as organs or lesions, and extract features for diagnosis. For instance, convolutional neural networks (CNNs) have been used for segmenting lung nodules in CT scans for early detection of lung cancer.

- Computer-aided detection and diagnosis (CAD): Machine learning algorithms can help radiologists detect abnormalities and diagnose diseases in medical images. For instance, CAD systems have been developed for detecting breast cancer in mammography images and identifying diabetic retinopathy in fundus photographs.

- Image classification: Machine learning algorithms can classify medical images into various categories based on the presence or absence of certain features. For instance, deep learning algorithms have been used for classifying skin lesions into benign or malignant categories in dermoscopy images.

2. Challenges of ML in Diagnostic Imaging

Although machine learning has shown great promise in diagnostic imaging, there are also several challenges that need to be addressed:

- Data availability and quality: Machine learning algorithms require large amounts of high-quality data for training and validation. However, medical imaging datasets are often small and imbalanced, which can affect the performance and generalizability of the models.

- Interpretability and explainability: Machine learning algorithms are often seen as black boxes, and it is difficult to understand how they arrive at their predictions. This lack of interpretability and explainability can make it difficult for clinicians to trust the results and integrate them into their clinical decision-making.

- Integration with clinical workflows: Machine learning algorithms need to be seamlessly integrated into clinical workflows to ensure that they are used effectively and efficiently. However, integrating new technologies into existing healthcare systems can be challenging, and it requires collaboration between clinicians, IT specialists, and other stakeholders.

3. Future Possibilities of ML in Diagnostic Imaging

Despite the challenges, machine learning has the potential to revolutionize diagnostic imaging and improve patient outcomes. Some of the future possibilities of machine learning in diagnostic imaging are:

- Personalized medicine: Machine learning algorithms can help tailor medical imaging to individual patients and their specific needs, such as optimizing imaging protocols, minimizing radiation exposure, and reducing false positives and false negatives.

- Multi-modal imaging: Machine learning algorithms can integrate multiple types of medical imaging to provide a more comprehensive and accurate diagnosis. For instance, combining MRI and positron emission tomography (PET) can improve the diagnosis of brain tumors.

- Real-time diagnosis: Machine learning algorithms can provide real-time diagnosis and decision support during medical procedures, such as surgery or interventional radiology.

In conclusion, machine learning has shown great promise in diagnostic imaging and has the potential to significantly improve the accuracy and speed of diagnosis, reduce errors and variability, and enhance patient outcomes. However, there are also several challenges that need to be addressed, such as data availability and quality, interpretability and explainability, and integration with clinical workflows. With further research and development, machine learning has the potential to revolutionize diagnostic imaging and transform healthcare.

Machine learning in pathology and dermatology

Machine learning (ML) is making significant progress in the diagnosis of diseases in the fields of pathology and dermatology. These fields rely on visual data and pattern recognition, making them well-suited for ML applications. ML has been used to identify cancerous cells, classify skin diseases, and even predict the likelihood of disease recurrence.

In pathology, ML algorithms can analyze images of tissue samples to identify and classify cancerous cells. These algorithms use computer vision techniques to recognize patterns in the images, such as the size and shape of cells, and use this information to make a diagnosis. One example of an ML application in pathology is the development of a model that uses deep learning to classify breast cancer in histopathology images with an accuracy of 92%.

Dermatology is another field where ML is showing great potential. Skin diseases can be difficult to diagnose, with many conditions sharing similar symptoms. ML algorithms can analyze images of skin lesions and classify them into different categories, such as benign or malignant. One example of an ML application in dermatology is the use of convolutional neural networks (CNNs) to diagnose melanoma, a type of skin cancer. In a study, CNNs were able to diagnose melanoma with an accuracy of 91%, outperforming dermatologists.

ML can also be used to predict the likelihood of disease recurrence in both pathology and dermatology. By analyzing images of tissue samples or skin lesions, ML algorithms can identify features that are predictive of recurrence and use them to make a prediction. This can help clinicians to decide on the most appropriate course of treatment for a patient.

However, there are also challenges to using ML in pathology and dermatology. One major challenge is the need for high-quality data to train the algorithms. ML algorithms rely on large datasets to learn patterns and make accurate predictions, but obtaining such datasets can be difficult in these fields. Another challenge is the need for interpretability, as it is important for clinicians to understand how an algorithm arrived at a diagnosis in order to make informed decisions.

Despite these challenges, ML is showing great promise in the fields of pathology and dermatology, and is expected to play an increasingly important role in the diagnosis and treatment of diseases in these areas.

Applications in predicting and diagnosing disease

Machine learning algorithms have shown promise in predicting and diagnosing various diseases, including cancer, cardiovascular disease, and diabetes. In this section, we will explore some of the applications of machine learning in predicting and diagnosing disease.

1. Cancer Diagnosis Machine learning algorithms have been used to improve the accuracy of cancer diagnosis. For example, researchers have used machine learning algorithms to analyze mammograms and identify suspicious lesions. In one study, a deep learning algorithm achieved a diagnostic accuracy of 94.5% in detecting breast cancer from mammograms, which was higher than that of radiologists (1). Machine learning algorithms have also been used to predict the risk of cancer in patients. For example, a study used machine learning algorithms to predict the risk of breast cancer recurrence in patients, which could help guide treatment decisions (2).

2. Cardiovascular Disease Diagnosis Machine learning algorithms have also been used to improve the accuracy of cardiovascular disease diagnosis. For example, researchers have used machine learning algorithms to analyze electrocardiogram (ECG) signals and identify patients at high risk of cardiovascular disease. In one study, a machine

learning algorithm achieved an accuracy of 90.2% in predicting cardiovascular disease risk from ECG signals (3). Machine learning algorithms have also been used to predict the risk of heart attack in patients. For example, a study used machine learning algorithms to predict the risk of heart attack in patients with diabetes, which could help guide preventive interventions (4).

3. Diabetes Diagnosis Machine learning algorithms have also been used to improve the accuracy of diabetes diagnosis. For example, researchers have used machine learning algorithms to analyze electronic health record data and identify patients at high risk of diabetes. In one study, a machine learning algorithm achieved an accuracy of 85.5% in predicting the risk of diabetes from electronic health record data (5). Machine learning algorithms have also been used to predict the risk of diabetic complications. For example, a study used machine learning algorithms to predict the risk of diabetic retinopathy, which could help guide screening and treatment decisions (6).

4. Limitations and Challenges While machine learning algorithms have shown promise in predicting and diagnosing disease, there are still several limitations and challenges that need to be addressed. One limitation is the lack of large, high-quality datasets for training and testing machine

learning algorithms. Another challenge is the interpretability of machine learning algorithms. As machine learning algorithms become more complex, it can be difficult to understand how they make their predictions. This can make it challenging for clinicians to trust and use these algorithms in clinical practice. Finally, there are also concerns about the potential for bias in machine learning algorithms, particularly if the algorithms are trained on biased datasets.

Despite these challenges, machine learning algorithms have the potential to significantly improve the accuracy and efficiency of disease diagnosis. With continued research and development, machine learning algorithms may become a valuable tool for clinicians in the diagnosis and management of a wide range of diseases.

Challenges and limitations of machine learning in diagnosis

Machine learning has shown great potential in aiding diagnosis, but it is not without its challenges and limitations. In this section, we will discuss some of the most significant obstacles facing the adoption of machine learning in diagnosis and highlight some of the limitations of the technology.

One of the most significant challenges of machine learning in diagnosis is the requirement for large, high-quality datasets. Machine learning models rely on vast amounts of data to accurately predict diagnoses. However, collecting and preparing these datasets can be challenging, especially in cases where data is siloed or fragmented. Additionally, it can be challenging to ensure that the data is clean and representative of the patient population.

Another challenge of machine learning in diagnosis is the issue of bias. Machine learning models are only as good as the data they are trained on, and if that data is biased in any way, it will impact the model's predictions. For example, if a model is trained on data that is predominantly from a particular demographic group, it may be less effective at predicting diagnoses in patients from other groups. Additionally, there is the risk of bias being introduced into the model during the feature selection process, where certain features are given more weight than others.

Interpretability is also a challenge in machine learning diagnosis. Machine learning models can be difficult to interpret, making it hard for doctors to understand how the model arrived at its diagnosis. This lack of transparency can make it challenging for physicians to trust the model's predictions, which is critical in diagnosis.

Finally, machine learning models can be prone to overfitting, where the model becomes too specialized to the training data and loses its ability to generalize to new data. Overfitting can occur when a model is too complex or when there is insufficient data to train the model effectively.

Despite these challenges, machine learning continues to hold great promise in the field of diagnosis. As we continue to address these challenges, we will see more widespread adoption of machine learning tools in the diagnostic process.

Chapter 4: Machine Learning Applications in Treatment

Personalized medicine and precision oncology

Introduction: Personalized medicine aims to tailor medical treatment to the individual characteristics of each patient, including their genetic makeup, lifestyle, and environment. Machine learning has emerged as a powerful tool to develop personalized treatment strategies in various medical fields, including oncology. Precision oncology, a subset of personalized medicine, involves using genomic data to match cancer patients with the most effective treatments. In this section, we will explore how machine learning is being used in personalized medicine and precision oncology, as well as the challenges and opportunities associated with this approach.

Machine Learning in Personalized Medicine: The concept of personalized medicine has been around for many years, but advances in genomics, electronic health records (EHRs), and machine learning have enabled healthcare providers to develop more accurate and effective treatment strategies for patients. Machine learning algorithms can be trained on large datasets of patient information, including genetic data, medical history, and lifestyle factors, to identify patterns and make predictions about a patient's disease risk, treatment response, and prognosis.

One example of machine learning in personalized medicine is the use of decision support tools to guide treatment decisions. These tools use algorithms to analyze patient data and provide recommendations for specific treatments or interventions. For instance, a machine learning algorithm may analyze a patient's genetic data to identify mutations that suggest a certain type of cancer, and recommend a targeted therapy that is known to be effective against that mutation.

Precision Oncology: Precision oncology is a rapidly evolving field that involves using genomic data to guide cancer treatment decisions. By analyzing a patient's tumor DNA, researchers can identify mutations or other genetic alterations that may be driving the cancer's growth. This information can then be used to match patients with targeted therapies that are designed to block the specific molecular pathways involved in their cancer.

Machine learning is a key tool in precision oncology, as it can help researchers to identify the genetic mutations that are most likely to respond to particular treatments. Machine learning algorithms can be trained on large datasets of genomic data and treatment outcomes to identify patterns and make predictions about which treatments are most likely to be effective for a given patient.

Challenges and Opportunities: Despite the promise of personalized medicine and precision oncology, there are still many challenges associated with implementing these approaches in clinical practice. One of the biggest challenges is the availability of high-quality data. Machine learning algorithms require large amounts of high-quality data to train effectively, and it can be difficult to obtain and manage these datasets.

Another challenge is the need for more sophisticated machine learning algorithms that can handle the complexity and variability of genomic data. Genomic data is highly dimensional and contains many different types of features, such as mutations, copy number variations, and gene expression levels. Machine learning algorithms must be able to handle this complexity and extract meaningful patterns from the data.

Despite these challenges, there are many opportunities for machine learning in personalized medicine and precision oncology. As more data becomes available, and algorithms become more sophisticated, we can expect to see more accurate and effective treatment strategies that are tailored to the individual needs of each patient. Machine learning is also likely to play a key role in drug discovery, as researchers use machine learning algorithms to identify new targets and develop more effective therapies.

Conclusion: Personalized medicine and precision oncology are exciting areas of research that have the potential to revolutionize the way we approach cancer treatment. Machine learning is a key tool in this effort, enabling researchers to analyze large amounts of data and develop more accurate and effective treatment strategies. However, there are still many challenges to be overcome, and more research is needed to fully realize the potential of these approaches. With continued innovation and collaboration between researchers, healthcare providers, and technology companies, we can expect to see significant progress in the field of personalized medicine and precision

Machine learning in drug discovery and development

Machine learning (ML) has tremendous potential in the field of drug discovery and development. The drug discovery process involves identifying and optimizing molecules that can target specific biological targets, and this process can take many years and cost billions of dollars. Machine learning can assist in this process by predicting the likelihood of success of a particular molecule, reducing the cost and time required for discovery and development.

One key area where machine learning has shown promise in drug discovery is in the prediction of drug-target interactions. In this approach, ML models are trained on large-scale chemical and biological data to predict which molecules are likely to interact with specific biological targets. By identifying these potential interactions, researchers can prioritize the most promising drug candidates for further testing.

Another area where machine learning can help is in the prediction of drug toxicity. Toxicity is a significant concern in drug development, and many potential drugs fail in clinical trials due to toxicity issues. Machine learning can assist in predicting the toxicity of a particular molecule by analyzing its chemical structure and identifying patterns that are associated with toxicity. This approach can help researchers identify and discard potentially toxic compounds early in the drug development process, saving time and resources.

Machine learning can also assist in optimizing the drug development process by predicting the most effective dosages for a particular drug. By analyzing large-scale patient data, machine learning models can predict the optimal dosages for a particular drug, taking into account factors such as patient age, weight, and medical history.

Precision medicine is an emerging field that aims to tailor medical treatment to an individual's specific genetic, environmental, and lifestyle factors. Machine learning can assist in this process by analyzing large-scale patient data to identify which treatments are most effective for specific patient subgroups. This approach can help improve treatment outcomes and reduce adverse effects.

One example of precision medicine in action is in the treatment of cancer. Machine learning models can analyze patient data to identify which treatments are most effective for specific types of cancer, taking into account factors such as tumor size, location, and genetic mutations. By tailoring treatments to the specific needs of each patient, precision oncology can help improve treatment outcomes and reduce the side effects associated with traditional cancer treatments.

Despite the tremendous potential of machine learning in drug discovery and development, there are also significant challenges and limitations. One major challenge is the lack of high-quality data, particularly in the early stages of drug development. Without sufficient data, machine learning models may not be able to accurately predict drug-target interactions or toxicity. Additionally, there are concerns about the interpretability and transparency of machine learning models in drug development. Given the high stakes involved in drug development, it is important that researchers can understand and explain the decisions made by these models.

Another significant limitation of machine learning in drug development is the lack of standardization in data collection and analysis. This can make it difficult to compare results across different studies and can lead to variability in the performance of machine learning models.

In conclusion, machine learning has the potential to revolutionize the field of drug discovery and development. By predicting drug-target interactions, toxicity, and optimal dosages, machine learning can help reduce the cost and time required for drug development and improve treatment outcomes for patients. However, significant challenges and limitations remain, and further research is needed to address these issues and maximize the potential of machine learning in this field.

Predicting treatment outcomes with machine learning

Machine learning algorithms are also being increasingly used to predict treatment outcomes for patients. This can help clinicians make more informed decisions about the most appropriate treatment for each individual patient, leading to improved patient outcomes and reduced healthcare costs.

Predictive modeling involves building a model that can predict a specific outcome based on input data. In healthcare, predictive models are used to predict a range of outcomes, including hospital readmission rates, patient mortality, and treatment outcomes.

One of the most significant challenges in predicting treatment outcomes is the vast amount of data involved. This includes a patient's medical history, genetic profile, lifestyle factors, and other data points. Machine learning algorithms are well-suited to handle this level of complexity and can identify patterns that might not be visible to humans.

Machine learning algorithms can also be used to predict the likelihood of a patient experiencing side effects from a particular treatment. This can help clinicians identify patients who may be at higher risk for adverse events and adjust their treatment plan accordingly.

In the field of oncology, machine learning algorithms are being used to predict treatment response and survival rates for cancer patients. For example, researchers at Memorial Sloan Kettering Cancer Center have developed a machine learning algorithm that can predict a patient's response to chemotherapy with a high degree of accuracy. The algorithm takes into account a range of factors, including the patient's age, gender, tumor size, and other clinical and genetic factors.

Similarly, machine learning algorithms are being used to predict the risk of relapse for patients with various types of cancer. For example, researchers at Stanford University developed a machine learning algorithm that can predict which breast cancer patients are at high risk of relapse after treatment. The algorithm takes into account a range of factors, including the patient's age, tumor size, hormone receptor status, and other clinical and genetic factors.

Another area where machine learning is being used to predict treatment outcomes is in mental health. Researchers at the University of Texas Southwestern Medical Center developed a machine learning algorithm that can predict which patients with depression are likely to respond best to different types of treatment. The algorithm takes into account a range of factors, including the patient's age, gender, symptom severity, and other clinical and demographic factors.

While there are many potential benefits to using machine learning to predict treatment outcomes, there are also some challenges and limitations. One of the biggest challenges is ensuring that the data used to train the algorithms is of high quality and accurately represents the population being studied. In addition, there are concerns about the potential for bias in the algorithms, which could lead to disparities in treatment outcomes for different patient groups.

Furthermore, machine learning algorithms may not always be able to provide a clear explanation of why a particular prediction was made. This can make it difficult for clinicians to understand how the algorithm arrived at its decision and may reduce their trust in the algorithm.

Despite these challenges, the potential benefits of using machine learning to predict treatment outcomes are significant. As the technology continues to improve and more data becomes available, we can expect to see an increasing number of applications of machine learning in this area.

Challenges and limitations of machine learning in treatment

While machine learning has shown great promise in various aspects of healthcare, including treatment, there are still several challenges and limitations that need to be addressed before it can be fully integrated into clinical practice. Here are some of the challenges and limitations of machine learning in treatment:

1. Lack of quality data: One of the biggest challenges in developing machine learning models for treatment is the availability and quality of data. Machine learning algorithms require large amounts of high-quality data to produce accurate results. However, healthcare data is often fragmented, incomplete, and of varying quality. This can make it difficult to develop accurate models, as well as to compare and validate results across different data sets.

2. Generalizability: Machine learning models are often developed and trained on specific patient populations and data sets. As a result, there is a risk of overfitting the model to the specific population, leading to poor generalizability to other patient populations. This can limit the usefulness and applicability of the model in clinical practice.

3. Interpretability: Machine learning models can often produce accurate results, but the inner workings of the

model are not always transparent or interpretable. This lack of interpretability can make it difficult to understand why the model produced a particular result or prediction, which can be a barrier to clinical acceptance and adoption.

4. Ethical and legal considerations: The use of machine learning in treatment raises several ethical and legal considerations, such as privacy, consent, and liability. For example, who is responsible if a machine learning model produces inaccurate results that lead to harm to a patient? These ethical and legal considerations must be addressed before machine learning can be fully integrated into clinical practice.

5. Integration with clinical workflows: Integrating machine learning models into clinical workflows can be a challenge. Healthcare providers are already overwhelmed with information and may not have the time or resources to review and interpret the results of a machine learning model. The design and implementation of machine learning models must take into account the clinical workflow and be user-friendly and efficient for healthcare providers to use.

6. Bias and fairness: Machine learning models can also be biased, leading to unfair or discriminatory outcomes. This can be particularly problematic in treatment, where the consequences of biased models can be life-altering. Bias can

arise from various sources, such as the quality and representativeness of the training data or the features used in the model. It is important to ensure that machine learning models are fair and unbiased and do not perpetuate existing health disparities.

7. Regulation: As with any new technology in healthcare, machine learning models will need to be regulated to ensure safety and effectiveness. Regulatory agencies such as the FDA are already grappling with how to regulate AI and machine learning in healthcare, and it is likely that additional regulations and guidelines will be developed as the technology continues to advance.

Conclusion

Machine learning has the potential to revolutionize treatment in healthcare, from personalized medicine to drug discovery to treatment outcomes prediction. However, there are also several challenges and limitations that need to be addressed before machine learning can be fully integrated into clinical practice. These challenges include the availability and quality of data, generalizability, interpretability, ethical and legal considerations, integration with clinical workflows, bias and fairness, and regulation. Addressing these challenges will require collaboration among healthcare providers, researchers, regulators, and policymakers, as well as ongoing innovation and advancement in machine learning technology.

Chapter 5: Machine Learning Applications in Healthcare Operations

Healthcare data management and analysis

Healthcare organizations are generating an enormous amount of data on a daily basis. Managing and analyzing this data is crucial to improve healthcare outcomes, reduce costs, and enhance patient satisfaction. The use of machine learning algorithms can help healthcare organizations to process and analyze these large datasets, leading to more informed decision-making.

In this section, we will discuss how machine learning is being used in healthcare data management and analysis.

Data Management

The first step in using machine learning for healthcare data analysis is to ensure the data is properly managed. This involves tasks such as data cleaning, data normalization, and data integration. Machine learning algorithms rely on high-quality, clean data to deliver accurate and reliable results. Some of the key ways machine learning is used in healthcare data management include:

1. Data preprocessing: Before data can be used for analysis, it needs to be cleaned and preprocessed. Machine learning algorithms can be used to automate this process,

ensuring that the data is properly formatted and any missing values are filled in.

2. Data integration: Healthcare data is often stored in different formats and systems. Machine learning algorithms can be used to integrate data from multiple sources, providing a more comprehensive view of patient health.

3. Data warehousing: Healthcare organizations often store large amounts of data in data warehouses. Machine learning algorithms can be used to process this data and provide insights that can help improve patient care and operational efficiency.

Data Analysis

Once the data is properly managed, it can be analyzed using machine learning algorithms to gain insights into patient health and improve healthcare outcomes. Some of the key ways machine learning is being used for healthcare data analysis include:

1. Predictive analytics: Machine learning algorithms can be used to analyze patient data to identify those who are at risk of developing certain conditions, allowing for earlier interventions and improved outcomes.

2. Clinical decision support: Machine learning algorithms can be used to provide decision support to

clinicians, helping them to make more informed decisions based on patient data.

3. Operational analytics: Machine learning algorithms can be used to analyze operational data to identify inefficiencies and improve operational efficiency.

4. Population health management: Machine learning algorithms can be used to analyze data at the population level, identifying trends and patterns that can help improve population health.

Challenges and Limitations

While machine learning has great potential in healthcare data management and analysis, there are also challenges and limitations to be aware of. Some of these challenges include:

1. Data quality: Machine learning algorithms rely on high-quality data to provide accurate and reliable results. Poor quality data can lead to inaccurate results and incorrect decisions.

2. Data privacy and security: Healthcare data is highly sensitive, and there are strict regulations governing its use and storage. Healthcare organizations must take steps to ensure data privacy and security when using machine learning algorithms.

3. Interpretability: Machine learning algorithms can be complex, making it difficult to interpret the results. Healthcare organizations must be able to explain the algorithms and results to stakeholders to gain their trust and support.

4. Bias: Machine learning algorithms can be biased if they are trained on biased data. Healthcare organizations must take steps to ensure that their data is unbiased and that algorithms are trained on a diverse range of data.

Conclusion

Machine learning is being used to manage and analyze healthcare data, leading to improved patient outcomes and operational efficiency. Proper data management is essential to ensure accurate and reliable results, and machine learning algorithms can help healthcare organizations to process and analyze large datasets. However, there are also challenges and limitations to be aware of, including data quality, privacy and security, interpretability, and bias. Healthcare organizations must take steps to address these challenges to fully realize the potential of machine learning in healthcare data management and analysis.

Streamlining clinical workflows with machine learning

In recent years, healthcare organizations have increasingly turned to machine learning to streamline clinical workflows and improve operational efficiency. Machine learning algorithms can help automate repetitive tasks, identify inefficiencies, and improve patient outcomes. In this chapter, we will explore the various ways in which machine learning is being applied to healthcare operations.

One of the most significant challenges faced by healthcare organizations is the sheer volume of data generated by clinical workflows. Machine learning can help to analyze and manage this data, enabling healthcare professionals to make more informed decisions. For example, machine learning algorithms can be trained on large volumes of patient data to identify patterns and insights that would be difficult to detect manually. This can help to improve diagnosis and treatment decisions and identify potential cost savings.

Another way in which machine learning is being used to streamline clinical workflows is through the automation of routine administrative tasks. For example, machine learning algorithms can be used to process and prioritize incoming patient information, such as lab results and medical imaging data. This can help to reduce the workload on healthcare professionals and ensure that patients receive timely and accurate care.

Machine learning is also being used to improve the scheduling and coordination of clinical workflows. By analyzing historical patient data, machine learning algorithms can predict the likelihood of patient cancellations and no-shows. This can help healthcare organizations to better allocate resources and reduce wait times for patients. Similarly, machine learning can be used to optimize staff schedules and ensure that the right healthcare professionals are available to meet patient needs.

Another area in which machine learning is being applied to healthcare operations is in the management of healthcare supply chains. By analyzing data on inventory levels, demand patterns, and supplier performance, machine learning algorithms can help healthcare organizations to optimize their supply chain operations. This can help to reduce costs, improve the quality of care, and minimize waste.

Despite the potential benefits of machine learning in healthcare operations, there are also significant challenges and limitations to its use. One challenge is the need for high-quality data to train machine learning algorithms.

Healthcare data is often complex and heterogeneous, making it difficult to integrate and analyze. Additionally, there are concerns about the privacy and security of patient data, which must be carefully managed to ensure compliance with regulations and ethical guidelines.

Another challenge is the potential for bias in machine learning algorithms. Bias can arise if the data used to train the algorithm is not representative of the broader population, leading to inaccurate or unfair predictions. This is particularly concerning in healthcare, where biased algorithms could lead to inequitable treatment and poorer patient outcomes.

In conclusion, machine learning has the potential to transform healthcare operations by improving efficiency, reducing costs, and improving patient outcomes. By analyzing and managing large volumes of healthcare data, automating routine tasks, and optimizing supply chain operations, machine learning can help healthcare organizations to deliver high-quality care to patients. However, there are also significant challenges and limitations to its use, including the need for high-quality data, concerns about bias, and the need to ensure patient privacy and security.

Predictive maintenance in medical equipment

Medical equipment plays a vital role in providing quality healthcare to patients. In healthcare facilities, there is an abundance of equipment that needs to be monitored and maintained regularly to ensure they are working correctly. If a piece of medical equipment breaks down, it can affect patient care and can even result in patient harm or death. Therefore, it is essential to have a system that can predict equipment failures and prevent them from happening in the first place. This is where machine learning comes into play. In this section, we will discuss how machine learning can be used for predictive maintenance in medical equipment and its benefits.

Predictive Maintenance:

Predictive maintenance is a process that uses machine learning algorithms to predict equipment failure before it occurs. In traditional maintenance practices, equipment is maintained on a schedule, which may not take into account the actual condition of the equipment. This can lead to unnecessary maintenance or equipment failure due to lack of maintenance. Predictive maintenance, on the other hand, uses real-time data to identify potential equipment problems and schedule maintenance before a failure occurs.

Benefits of Predictive Maintenance:

There are many benefits of using predictive maintenance for medical equipment. Some of the most significant benefits are:

1. Reduced downtime: Predictive maintenance allows for scheduled maintenance to be performed before equipment failure occurs, reducing the amount of downtime due to equipment failure.

2. Cost savings: By preventing equipment failure, healthcare facilities can save money on repairs and replacements, as well as reduce the cost of emergency repairs.

3. Improved patient care: Predictive maintenance ensures that equipment is in good working order, reducing the risk of equipment failure during patient care and improving patient outcomes.

4. Increased equipment lifespan: Regular maintenance can extend the life of medical equipment, reducing the need for costly replacements.

5. Efficient use of resources: Predictive maintenance allows healthcare facilities to allocate their resources more efficiently by focusing on equipment that needs maintenance rather than maintaining all equipment on a schedule.

Challenges of Predictive Maintenance:

Although there are many benefits to predictive maintenance, there are also some challenges that need to be addressed. Some of the most significant challenges are:

1. Data collection: Predictive maintenance requires large amounts of data to be collected and analyzed. This can be challenging in healthcare facilities, where data is often scattered across multiple systems.

2. Data quality: The accuracy of predictive maintenance relies on the quality of the data used. In healthcare, data quality can be an issue due to the complexity of the systems and the variety of data sources.

3. Integration with existing systems: Integrating predictive maintenance with existing healthcare systems can be challenging, as it requires compatibility with multiple systems and data formats.

4. Staff training: Healthcare staff need to be trained on the use of predictive maintenance systems and how to interpret the data generated.

Applications of Predictive Maintenance:

Predictive maintenance can be applied to a wide range of medical equipment, including:

1. Imaging equipment: MRI machines, CT scanners, and X-ray machines are all critical pieces of medical

equipment that need to be maintained regularly to ensure they are in good working order.

2. Life support equipment: Ventilators, anesthesia machines, and dialysis machines are just a few examples of life support equipment that need to be maintained to ensure patient safety.

3. Laboratory equipment: Medical laboratories rely on a variety of equipment, including microscopes, centrifuges, and spectrophotometers, all of which need to be maintained to ensure accurate test results.

4. Patient monitoring equipment: Patient monitors, ECG machines, and blood pressure monitors are just a few examples of patient monitoring equipment that need to be maintained to ensure accurate readings.

In conclusion, predictive maintenance using machine learning can help healthcare facilities reduce downtime, save costs, improve patient care, and increase the lifespan of medical equipment. However, there are also challenges that need to be addressed, such as the need for high-quality data and expertise in machine learning algorithms. Additionally, there may be concerns about the potential for false alarms or missed failures, which could lead to safety issues. It is important for healthcare facilities to carefully evaluate the benefits and risks of implementing predictive maintenance with machine learning and ensure proper training and ongoing maintenance of the algorithms. With proper planning and execution, predictive maintenance using machine learning has the potential to revolutionize the way healthcare facilities manage their equipment and ultimately improve patient outcomes.

Another area where machine learning is being applied in healthcare operations is in supply chain management. The healthcare supply chain is complex, with multiple stakeholders involved in the sourcing, transportation, and delivery of products and services. Machine learning algorithms can help optimize supply chain operations by analyzing data on factors such as inventory levels, demand patterns, and delivery times. This can lead to more efficient ordering, reduced waste, and improved patient care. However, challenges such as data quality and data privacy must be addressed to ensure successful implementation of machine learning in supply chain management.

Challenges and limitations of machine learning in healthcare operations

Machine learning (ML) has shown great potential in improving healthcare operations, but as with any technology, it has its limitations and challenges. In this section, we will discuss some of the main challenges and limitations of ML in healthcare operations.

1. Data Quality and Quantity:

One of the primary challenges of machine learning in healthcare operations is data quality and quantity. ML algorithms require large amounts of high-quality data to be effective, and in many cases, the data available is incomplete, inconsistent, or of poor quality. Moreover, data privacy regulations, such as the Health Insurance Portability and Accountability Act (HIPAA) in the United States, can limit access to data that is critical for ML applications.

2. Integration with Existing Systems:

Another challenge is the integration of ML algorithms into existing healthcare systems. Many healthcare organizations still rely on legacy systems that may not be compatible with newer technologies. Moreover, integrating ML algorithms into existing systems requires expertise in both machine learning and healthcare IT, which can be hard to come by.

3. Bias in Data and Algorithms:

Machine learning algorithms are only as good as the data they are trained on. If the data used to train the algorithm is biased, the algorithm will also be biased. Moreover, there is a risk that the algorithm itself may introduce bias, particularly if the data is not representative of the population being served.

4. Regulatory and Ethical Concerns:

As with any technology, there are also regulatory and ethical concerns surrounding the use of machine learning in healthcare operations. For example, if an ML algorithm is used to triage patients, there is a risk that patients may be denied care based on the algorithm's output. Similarly, there are concerns about the ethical implications of using ML algorithms to make decisions about patient care.

5. Technical Complexity:

Implementing and maintaining machine learning algorithms can be technically complex. Healthcare organizations may not have the expertise or resources needed to build and maintain these systems in-house. Moreover, ML algorithms require a significant amount of computational power, which can be expensive to acquire and maintain.

6. Lack of Transparency:

Finally, one of the challenges of machine learning in healthcare operations is the lack of transparency in the algorithms used. Many ML algorithms are black boxes, meaning that it is difficult to understand how they arrive at their decisions. This lack of transparency can be a concern, particularly when it comes to making decisions about patient care.

In conclusion, while machine learning has the potential to revolutionize healthcare operations, there are also significant challenges and limitations that need to be addressed. Addressing these challenges will require collaboration between healthcare organizations, machine learning experts, and regulatory bodies to ensure that the benefits of this technology are realized while minimizing the risks.

Chapter 6: The Future of AI in Medicine
Current and potential future AI applications in medicine

Artificial intelligence (AI) has made significant progress in healthcare, and there are numerous current and potential future applications for AI in medicine. In this section, we will explore some of the current and potential future AI applications in medicine.

One of the current applications of AI in medicine is in medical imaging. AI algorithms can analyze medical images to detect anomalies, classify diseases, and aid in treatment planning. AI can also help radiologists to identify subtle patterns in medical images that are difficult for the human eye to see, leading to more accurate and faster diagnoses.

Another area where AI is currently being used in medicine is in drug discovery. AI can help identify new drug targets, design new molecules, and optimize clinical trials. AI algorithms can also help predict the efficacy and toxicity of drugs, which can speed up the drug discovery process and save costs.

AI is also being used in precision medicine, which aims to customize treatments for individual patients based on their unique characteristics. AI algorithms can analyze a patient's medical history, genetics, and lifestyle to identify the most effective treatment options for that patient.

In addition to these current applications, there are many potential future applications of AI in medicine. For example, AI could be used to predict and prevent disease before symptoms appear. AI algorithms can analyze large amounts of data to identify patterns and risk factors that are not immediately apparent, allowing for earlier interventions and prevention.

AI could also be used to create more personalized treatment plans. By analyzing patient data, including genetics, medical history, and lifestyle, AI algorithms can identify the best treatment options for each patient, taking into account their individual characteristics.

AI could also be used to monitor patients remotely, allowing for earlier intervention in case of any changes in their health. This could help reduce hospital readmissions and improve patient outcomes.

Another potential future application of AI in medicine is in robotic surgery. Robots can perform surgeries with greater precision and accuracy than human surgeons, reducing the risk of complications and allowing for faster recovery times.

Overall, AI has the potential to revolutionize medicine by improving diagnosis, treatment, and patient outcomes. However, there are also challenges and limitations that need to be addressed, including data privacy and security, regulatory hurdles, and ensuring that AI is used ethically and responsibly. Nevertheless, the potential benefits of AI in medicine are immense, and we can expect to see continued growth and development in this field in the coming years.

The role of AI in transforming healthcare

Artificial intelligence (AI) has the potential to revolutionize healthcare by transforming the way we diagnose, treat, and prevent diseases. With its ability to analyze large amounts of data quickly and accurately, AI can help healthcare professionals make more informed decisions, improve patient outcomes, and reduce costs. Here, we will discuss the role of AI in transforming healthcare, including its current and potential future applications.

One of the most significant ways that AI is transforming healthcare is by improving diagnostic accuracy. Machine learning algorithms can analyze medical images, such as X-rays and MRIs, and identify abnormalities that may be missed by human radiologists. AI can also analyze large amounts of patient data, such as electronic health records (EHRs), to identify patterns and predict diseases earlier. This can lead to earlier diagnoses, more personalized treatments, and ultimately better outcomes for patients.

AI can also help to streamline healthcare operations and reduce costs. For example, AI-powered chatbots can provide patients with personalized information and support, reducing the need for in-person visits. Machine learning algorithms can also help to optimize hospital staffing and bed allocation, reducing wait times and increasing efficiency.

AI can even help to identify potential fraud and abuse in healthcare billing, saving money and improving the overall quality of care.

Another area where AI is transforming healthcare is in drug discovery and development. By analyzing vast amounts of data on potential drug compounds, AI can help to identify promising candidates faster and more efficiently than traditional methods. This can lead to the development of more effective and targeted drugs, as well as faster approvals by regulatory agencies.

Looking to the future, AI has the potential to revolutionize healthcare even further. One exciting area of research is the development of AI-powered robotic assistants, which can perform surgery and other medical procedures with greater precision and accuracy than human doctors. AI can also help to develop more personalized treatments, by analyzing patient data and tailoring treatments to individual needs. AI-powered wearable devices, such as smart watches, can continuously monitor vital signs and provide real-time feedback to patients and healthcare professionals.

However, there are also challenges and potential limitations to the use of AI in healthcare. One major concern is the potential for bias in AI algorithms, which can lead to inaccurate diagnoses and treatments. To address this, it is important to ensure that AI algorithms are trained on diverse and representative datasets. Another concern is the need to protect patient privacy and data security, as large amounts of sensitive medical data are being collected and analyzed by AI systems.

In conclusion, the role of AI in transforming healthcare is rapidly expanding. From improving diagnostic accuracy to streamlining operations and drug development, AI has the potential to revolutionize the way we deliver and receive healthcare. While there are challenges and potential limitations, continued research and development in this field will lead to a future where AI and human healthcare professionals work together to provide the best possible care for patients.

Ethical and social considerations in AI in medicine

Artificial intelligence (AI) has the potential to transform healthcare, from personalized medicine to improved patient outcomes and operational efficiencies. However, as with any new technology, there are ethical and social considerations that must be addressed to ensure that AI is used in a responsible and ethical manner. In this section, we will discuss some of the ethical and social considerations in AI in medicine.

1. Data Privacy and Security:

Data privacy and security are critical considerations in any healthcare technology, including AI. Healthcare data is highly sensitive and must be protected from unauthorized access or disclosure. AI systems that use personal health information must comply with relevant data privacy regulations, such as the Health Insurance Portability and Accountability Act (HIPAA) in the United States.

Moreover, AI systems can potentially identify individuals through data processing and analysis, even if the data is anonymized. Therefore, it is important to ensure that AI systems are designed to protect the privacy and confidentiality of individuals' health information.

2. Bias and Fairness:

One of the major concerns with AI in medicine is the potential for bias and unfairness. AI algorithms are only as unbiased as the data they are trained on. If the training data is biased, the AI system will also be biased, leading to inaccurate or unfair predictions and decisions.

Moreover, AI systems can perpetuate existing biases in healthcare, such as racial or gender biases. For example, a study found that an AI system used to predict healthcare needs in a population with chronic illness showed bias towards white patients, resulting in lower healthcare utilization rates for non-white patients.

To address this issue, it is important to ensure that the data used to train AI systems is diverse and representative of the population, and that the AI algorithms are designed to be transparent and auditable, so that any biases can be identified and addressed.

3. Accountability and Responsibility:

Another consideration in AI in medicine is accountability and responsibility. As AI systems become more complex and autonomous, it can be difficult to assign responsibility for any errors or adverse outcomes. It is important to establish clear lines of responsibility and accountability for AI systems, including the developers, operators, and users.

Moreover, there is a risk that AI systems could be used to replace human judgement and decision-making entirely, leading to potential legal and ethical issues. Therefore, it is important to ensure that AI systems are designed to augment human decision-making, rather than replace it entirely.

4. Transparency and Explainability:

Transparency and explainability are critical considerations in AI in medicine. It is important to ensure that AI systems are designed to be transparent and explainable, so that users can understand how the system works and how decisions are made.

Moreover, patients and healthcare providers need to be able to trust the AI systems they use. Transparency and explainability can help to build trust and ensure that AI systems are used in a responsible and ethical manner.

5. Societal Impacts:

AI in medicine can have significant societal impacts, including changes to the healthcare workforce and access to healthcare. AI has the potential to automate many routine healthcare tasks, such as administrative tasks or data entry, which could free up healthcare professionals to focus on more complex tasks.

However, there is a risk that AI could lead to job losses in the healthcare sector, particularly for low-skilled workers. Therefore, it is important to consider the potential societal impacts of AI in medicine and to develop strategies to mitigate any negative impacts.

Conclusion:

AI has the potential to transform healthcare, but it also raises ethical and social considerations that must be addressed. Data privacy and security, bias and fairness, accountability and responsibility, transparency and explainability, and societal impacts are critical considerations in AI in medicine. By addressing these considerations, we can ensure that AI is used in a responsible and ethical manner, to improve patient outcomes and transform healthcare for the better.

Opportunities and challenges in future AI development in medicine

Artificial Intelligence (AI) has already shown great promise in transforming the field of medicine, and it is expected to play an even more significant role in the future. AI has the potential to revolutionize the entire healthcare system, from the way medical research is conducted, to the way diagnoses are made and treatments are prescribed. In this section, we will discuss the opportunities and challenges associated with the future development of AI in medicine.

Opportunities:

1. Improved diagnostics and personalized medicine: AI can analyze vast amounts of medical data and identify patterns and correlations that may not be immediately apparent to human clinicians. This can lead to more accurate and timely diagnoses, and the development of personalized treatment plans tailored to an individual patient's unique genetic makeup.

2. Drug discovery and development: AI can help identify new drug candidates and optimize existing ones. By analyzing large datasets, AI algorithms can identify potential targets for drug development, predict the efficacy of new drugs, and even simulate the clinical trial process, reducing the time and cost of bringing new drugs to market.

3. Remote monitoring and telemedicine: AI can be used to remotely monitor patients and identify potential health problems before they become serious. This can be particularly useful for patients with chronic conditions or those living in remote areas without easy access to healthcare facilities. Telemedicine can also provide patients with access to medical experts from all over the world, improving the quality of care and reducing costs.

4. Healthcare operations: AI can be used to optimize healthcare operations, from scheduling appointments to managing medical records. By automating routine tasks, healthcare providers can save time and focus on providing better patient care.

Challenges:

1. Data privacy and security: The use of AI in medicine relies heavily on the collection and analysis of patient data, which raises concerns about privacy and security. Measures must be put in place to protect sensitive patient information from unauthorized access and use.

2. Regulatory issues: The development and deployment of AI in medicine is subject to regulatory oversight, which can be complex and time-consuming. The regulatory framework must be carefully designed to ensure that AI is used ethically and safely.

3. Bias and fairness: AI algorithms can perpetuate existing biases and inequalities if they are trained on biased data or are not designed to account for ethical considerations. It is essential to ensure that AI systems are fair and unbiased, and that they do not perpetuate discrimination.

4. Technical challenges: Developing effective AI systems for healthcare is challenging, as they must be able to handle complex data and operate in real-time. AI systems must also be designed to work seamlessly with existing healthcare technologies and workflows.

Conclusion:

The future of AI in medicine is full of promise, but it also poses significant challenges. To fully realize the potential of AI in healthcare, it is essential to address these challenges proactively and develop ethical, fair, and effective AI systems that can help transform the healthcare industry for the better. By collaborating with healthcare professionals, patients, and regulators, we can develop AI systems that are safe, effective, and equitable, and that can help us provide better healthcare to everyone.

Conclusion
The potential of AI in transforming healthcare

The rapid advancement of Artificial Intelligence (AI) has led to significant progress in various fields, including healthcare. The use of AI in medicine has shown immense potential in transforming the way healthcare is delivered. The integration of AI technologies in healthcare can enhance disease diagnosis, treatment, and prevention, as well as streamline healthcare operations.

One of the most significant benefits of AI in healthcare is the potential for earlier and more accurate disease diagnosis. With the help of AI, healthcare professionals can analyze vast amounts of patient data to identify patterns and predict the likelihood of a disease or illness developing. Machine learning algorithms can analyze medical images such as CT scans, MRI scans, and X-rays to identify potential health risks accurately. In addition, AI can also be used to monitor and track patients' vital signs and detect early warning signs of health problems, thereby allowing for early intervention and treatment.

The use of AI in drug discovery and development is another promising application. AI can analyze large amounts of data to identify potential drug targets, predict the efficacy of drug candidates, and even design new drugs. This can significantly reduce the time and cost associated with traditional drug discovery methods, leading to faster and more effective treatments for patients.

Furthermore, AI can improve personalized medicine and precision oncology, which tailors treatments to individual patients based on their unique genetic makeup, medical history, and lifestyle. This approach can lead to more effective treatments with fewer side effects, ultimately improving patient outcomes.

AI can also optimize healthcare operations by streamlining clinical workflows, automating administrative tasks, and predicting equipment failures. This can reduce the burden on healthcare professionals, improve patient care, and save costs for healthcare facilities.

Despite the significant potential of AI in healthcare, several challenges and limitations need to be addressed. These include the need for extensive training data, regulatory challenges, and concerns around privacy and ethics. Additionally, there is a risk of AI perpetuating biases and exacerbating health disparities if not carefully monitored and regulated.

As the field of AI in medicine continues to advance, it is essential to consider the opportunities and challenges that come with this technology. The development of ethical guidelines and regulations is crucial to ensure that AI is used safely and equitably in healthcare. Collaborations between healthcare professionals, researchers, and industry experts are also essential to develop and implement AI solutions that address the most pressing healthcare challenges.

In conclusion, AI has significant potential in transforming healthcare and improving patient outcomes. The use of AI technologies in healthcare can enhance disease diagnosis, treatment, and prevention, as well as streamline healthcare operations. While there are challenges and limitations, these can be addressed through collaboration, innovation, and ethical considerations. As the field of AI in medicine continues to evolve, it is essential to harness its potential to improve healthcare outcomes and promote global health equity.

The need for continued research and development in AI in medicine

Artificial intelligence (AI) has made significant advancements in the field of medicine in recent years, with applications in diagnosis, treatment, and healthcare operations. However, the potential for AI to transform healthcare is still largely untapped, and continued research and development in this area is necessary to fully realize its benefits.

One area where continued research is needed is in improving the accuracy and reliability of AI models. While AI has shown promising results in many applications, there are still limitations and challenges that need to be addressed. For example, AI models can be susceptible to bias, particularly if they are trained on biased datasets. Additionally, AI models can struggle with understanding context and making accurate predictions in complex situations.

Another area where continued research is needed is in expanding the applications of AI in healthcare. While AI has already shown promise in several areas, there are many other areas of medicine where it has yet to be fully explored. For example, AI could be used to improve patient monitoring, to predict and prevent adverse events, and to develop new therapies and treatments.

Additionally, the ethical and social implications of AI in medicine need to be carefully considered and addressed. For example, there are concerns about the potential for AI to be used to replace human healthcare professionals, or to be used in ways that could infringe on patient privacy or autonomy. These concerns need to be carefully addressed through careful regulation and ethical guidelines.

Overall, continued research and development in AI in medicine is essential for unlocking the full potential of this technology. By addressing the challenges and limitations of current AI models, expanding the applications of AI in healthcare, and carefully considering the ethical and social implications of AI, we can work towards a future where AI is an integral part of healthcare delivery, improving outcomes for patients and healthcare professionals alike.

The importance of ethical and responsible AI development and use in healthcare

The integration of AI in healthcare has the potential to revolutionize the industry and improve patient outcomes. However, as AI technology becomes more advanced and ubiquitous, it is important to consider the ethical and responsible development and use of these systems in healthcare. In this section, we will explore the importance of ethical and responsible AI development and use in healthcare and the potential risks and challenges associated with the use of AI in healthcare.

The Risks and Challenges of AI in Healthcare: As AI systems become more advanced and integrated into healthcare, it is important to consider the potential risks and challenges associated with their use. One of the most significant risks is the potential for bias in AI algorithms. AI systems learn from data, and if that data is biased, the resulting algorithms will also be biased. This can result in unequal treatment of patients, particularly for marginalized groups who may be underrepresented in the data used to train these systems. Another potential risk is the potential for errors or malfunctions in AI systems, which can lead to misdiagnosis, incorrect treatment recommendations, or other harmful outcomes. It is also important to consider the potential impact of AI on healthcare workers, particularly in terms of job displacement and changing roles and responsibilities.

Ethical and Responsible AI Development and Use: To address these risks and challenges, it is essential to ensure the ethical and responsible development and use of AI in healthcare. This includes considering the potential biases in data used to train these systems and taking steps to mitigate those biases. It also means developing transparent and explainable AI systems that can be audited and validated to ensure their accuracy and reliability. It is important to prioritize patient safety and well-being over profit or other interests, and to ensure that AI systems are developed in collaboration with healthcare professionals and patients to ensure their effectiveness and appropriateness. Additionally, it is essential to consider the potential impact of AI on healthcare workers and to provide training and support to help them adapt to changing roles and responsibilities.

Conclusion: AI has the potential to transform healthcare by improving patient outcomes, increasing efficiency, and reducing costs. However, it is important to consider the ethical and responsible development and use of these systems in healthcare to minimize risks and ensure that patient safety and well-being are prioritized. This requires collaboration between AI developers, healthcare professionals, and patients to ensure that AI systems are developed and used in a manner that aligns with the values of the healthcare industry and benefits all stakeholders. As AI technology continues to evolve and become more integrated into healthcare, it is important to prioritize responsible and ethical development and use to ensure that these systems are beneficial and effective tools for improving patient care.

Final thoughts and recommendations for further reading

As AI continues to evolve and transform healthcare, it is important to stay informed and up-to-date on the latest developments and best practices in the field. In this section, we will provide some final thoughts and recommendations for further reading.

First, it is clear that AI has tremendous potential to improve patient outcomes, reduce costs, and streamline healthcare operations. However, it is important to approach AI development and use with caution and responsibility. As discussed earlier in this book, there are ethical and social considerations to take into account when developing and using AI in healthcare. We must strive to ensure that AI is developed and used in ways that are fair, transparent, and accountable, and that respect patient privacy and autonomy.

Second, it is important to acknowledge that AI is not a panacea for all healthcare problems. While AI has shown great promise in certain areas, it is not a replacement for human expertise and judgment. AI should be used as a tool to augment and support human decision-making, not replace it.

Third, as AI continues to evolve and become more integrated into healthcare systems, there is a need for continued research and development. We must strive to develop AI algorithms and tools that are more accurate, reliable, and robust, and that can adapt to new challenges and contexts.

Finally, we recommend further reading on the following topics:

1. Ethical and social considerations in AI development and use in healthcare, including issues of bias, fairness, transparency, and accountability.

2. The role of AI in improving patient outcomes, reducing costs, and streamlining healthcare operations, including case studies and real-world examples of successful AI applications.

3. The latest developments and best practices in AI algorithms and tools for diagnosis, treatment, and healthcare operations, including advances in deep learning, natural language processing, and data analytics.

4. The challenges and limitations of AI in healthcare, including issues of data quality, interoperability, and scalability, as well as the need for continued research and development.

In conclusion, AI has tremendous potential to transform healthcare and improve patient outcomes, but we must approach AI development and use with caution and responsibility. We must strive to ensure that AI is developed and used in ways that are fair, transparent, and accountable, and that respect patient privacy and autonomy. Further research and development is needed to improve the accuracy, reliability, and robustness of AI algorithms and tools, and to address the challenges and limitations of AI in healthcare. By staying informed and engaged in the latest developments and best practices in AI, we can help ensure that AI is used to its fullest potential in improving healthcare for all.

THE END

Glossary

Below are some key terms and definitions related to the topic of AI in medicine:

1. Artificial Intelligence (AI): The simulation of human intelligence processes by computer systems, including machine learning and natural language processing.

2. Machine Learning (ML): A type of AI that allows machines to learn from data, identify patterns, and make predictions or decisions without being explicitly programmed.

3. Deep Learning: A subset of machine learning that uses neural networks to identify complex patterns and relationships in data.

4. Natural Language Processing (NLP): The ability of machines to understand and interpret human language, including speech and text.

5. Electronic Health Record (EHR): A digital version of a patient's medical record that contains information on their health status, medical history, diagnoses, medications, and treatments.

6. Clinical Decision Support (CDS): A computerized system that provides healthcare professionals with information and recommendations to support clinical decision-making.

7. Predictive Analytics: The use of data, statistical algorithms, and machine learning techniques to identify the likelihood of future outcomes based on historical data.

8. Precision Medicine: An approach to patient care that takes into account individual variability in genes, environment, and lifestyle to tailor medical treatments to specific patients.

9. Personalized Medicine: A synonym for precision medicine that emphasizes the customization of medical care to individual patients.

10. Telemedicine: The use of technology, such as video conferencing and remote monitoring, to deliver medical care and services from a distance.

11. Big Data: Extremely large data sets that can be analyzed computationally to reveal patterns, trends, and associations.

12. Internet of Things (IoT): A network of physical objects embedded with sensors, software, and other technologies that enable them to collect and exchange data.

13. Augmented Reality (AR): A technology that overlays digital information and images onto the real world.

14. Virtual Reality (VR): A technology that creates a simulated environment, allowing users to interact with it as if it were real.

15. Ethics: A branch of philosophy that concerns moral principles and values, including the concepts of right and wrong, good and bad, and justice and fairness.

16. Bias: A systematic error or distortion in data or algorithms that can lead to unfair or inaccurate results.

17. Explainability: The ability of an AI system to provide clear and understandable explanations for its decisions or recommendations.

18. Transparency: The openness and accessibility of an AI system's data, algorithms, and decision-making processes.

19. Regulation: Rules and guidelines set by government bodies or other organizations to ensure the safe, ethical, and responsible development and use of AI in medicine.

20. Standardization: The process of establishing uniform procedures and protocols for the collection, management, and analysis of data in healthcare.

Potential References

Introduction:

Rajkomar, A., Dean, J., & Kohane, I. (2019). Machine learning in medicine. New England Journal of Medicine, 380(14), 1347-1358.

Topol, E. (2019). High-performance medicine: the convergence of human and artificial intelligence. Nature Medicine, 25(1), 44-56.

Beam, A. L., & Kohane, I. S. (2018). Big data and machine learning in health care. JAMA, 319(13), 1317-1318.

Chapter 1: The History of AI in Medicine:

Russell, S. J., & Norvig, P. (2010). Artificial intelligence: a modern approach (3rd ed.). Upper Saddle River, NJ: Prentice Hall.

Shortliffe, E. H., & Sepúlveda, M. J. (2018). Clinical decision support in the era of artificial intelligence. Journal of the American Medical Association, 320(21), 2199-2200.

Weng, S. F., Reps, J., Kai, J., Garibaldi, J. M., & Qureshi, N. (2017). Can machine-learning improve cardiovascular risk prediction using routine clinical data? PLoS One, 12(4), e0174944.

Chapter 2: Machine Learning Fundamentals:

Alpaydin, E. (2010). Introduction to machine learning (2nd ed.). Cambridge, MA: MIT Press.

Bishop, C. M. (2006). Pattern recognition and machine learning (1st ed.). New York: Springer.

Murphy, K. P. (2012). Machine learning: a probabilistic perspective. Cambridge, MA: MIT Press.

Chapter 3: Machine Learning Applications in Diagnosis:
Esteva, A., Kuprel, B., Novoa, R. A., Ko, J., Swetter, S. M., Blau, H. M., & Thrun, S. (2017). Dermatologist-level classification of skin cancer with deep neural networks. Nature, 542(7639), 115-118.

Haenssle, H. A., Fink, C., Schneiderbauer, R., Toberer, F., Buhl, T., Blum, A., ... & Thomas, L. (2018). Man against machine: diagnostic performance of a deep learning convolutional neural network for dermoscopic melanoma recognition in comparison to 157 dermatologists. Annals of Oncology, 29(8), 1836-1842.

Litjens, G., Kooi, T., Bejnordi, B. E., Setio, A. A., Ciompi, F., Ghafoorian, M., ... & van Ginneken, B. (2017). A survey on deep learning in medical image analysis. Medical Image Analysis, 42, 60-88.

Chapter 4: Machine Learning Applications in Treatment
Torkamani, A., Andersen, K. G., Steinhubl, S. R., & Topol, E. J. (2017). High-definition medicine. Cell systems, 5(6), 611-617.

Gawehn, E., Hiss, J. A., & Schneider, G. (2016). Deep learning in drug discovery. Molecular informatics, 35(1), 3-14.

Chapter 5: Machine Learning Applications in Healthcare Operations

Chute, C. G., Beck, S. A., Fisk, T. B., & Mohr, D. N. (2016). The Enterprise Data Trust at Mayo Clinic: a semantically integrated warehouse of biomedical data. Journal of the American Medical Informatics Association, 23(3), 467-472.

Xie, B., He, D., Mercer, T., Wang, J., & Wu, D. (2019). Improving the prediction of hospital readmission among patients with heart failure using machine learning. Journal of the American Medical Informatics Association, 26(3), 206-212.

Chapter 6: The Future of AI in Medicine

Topol, E. J. (2019). High-performance medicine: the convergence of human and artificial intelligence. Nature Medicine, 25(1), 44-56. doi: 10.1038/s41591-018-0300-7

Wang, Y., Huang, C., Peng, Y., Liu, Z., & Lu, H. (2020). Applications of artificial intelligence in clinical medicine: advances and challenges. Journal of Healthcare Engineering, 2020, 1-12. doi: 10.1155/2020/2142627

Obermeyer, Z., & Emanuel, E. J. (2016). Predicting the future—big data, machine learning, and clinical medicine.

New England Journal of Medicine, 375(13), 1216-1219. doi: 10.1056/NEJMp1606181

Chen, J. H., Asch, S. M., & Machine Learning and Prediction in Medicine — Beyond the Peak of Inflated Expectations. The New England Journal of Medicine, 376(15), 1477-1479. doi: 10.1056/NEJMp1702071

Esteva, A., Robicquet, A., Ramsundar, B., Kuleshov, V., DePristo, M., Chou, K., ... & Dean, J. (2019). A guide to deep learning in healthcare. Nature Medicine, 25(1), 24-29. doi: 10.1038/s41591-018-0316-z

Wiens, J., & Shenoy, E. S. (2018). Machine learning for healthcare: on the verge of a major shift in healthcare epidemiology. Clinical Infectious Diseases, 66(1), 149-153. doi: 10.1093/cid/cix753

Char, D. S., Shah, N. H., Magnus, D., Mandl, K. D., & Hripcsak, G. (2018). Implementing machine learning in health care—addressing ethical challenges. New England Journal of Medicine, 378(11), 981-983. doi: 10.1056/NEJMp1714229

Darcy, A. M., Louie, A. K., Roberts, L. W., & Machine learning and the profession of medicine. JAMA, 315(6), 551-552. doi: 10.1001/jama.2015.18421

Rimmer, A. (2019). AI and machine learning are helping doctors but the key to success is partnership. BMJ, 364, l1092. doi: 10.1136/bmj.l1092

Brinker, T. J., Hekler, E. B., Thrul, J., Kreslake, J. M., & Schindler-Ruwisch, J. M. (2021). A novel approach to increasing engagement in internet interventions: a randomized controlled trial testing the integration of human support into an online smoking cessation program. Journal of medical Internet research, 23(1), e20068. doi: 10.2196/20068

Conclusion

Bresnick, J. (2020). The top 10 healthcare IT advances of the 2010s. HealthITAnalytics. Retrieved from https://healthitanalytics.com/features/the-top-10-healthcare-it-advances-of-the-2010s

Cho, S., Lee, J. H., & Kim, S. J. (2018). Potential of machine learning in clinical medicine and impact on cardiovascular risk prediction. Korean Circulation Journal, 48(8), 665-677. doi: 10.4070/kcj.2018.0247

European Commission. (2019). Ethics guidelines for trustworthy AI. Retrieved from https://ec.europa.eu/digital-single-market/en/news/ethics-guidelines-trustworthy-ai

Ghassemi, M. M., Naumann, T., Schulam, P., Beam, A. L., Chen, I. Y., Ranganath, R., & Ercole, A. (2018). A review of challenges and opportunities in machine learning for health. ACM Computing Surveys, 51(4), 1-36. doi: 10.1145/3234154

Harries, R. L., Schofield, D., & Callahan, A. (2019). Understanding the ethical implications of artificial intelligence in radiology. Journal of the American College of Radiology, 16(2), 168-176. doi: 10.1016/j.jacr.2018.09.034

Khairat, S., Liu, S., Zaman, T., & Edson, B. (2019). Artificial intelligence in healthcare: Past, present and future. American Journal of Medicine, 132(7), 795-801. doi: 10.1016/j.amjmed.2019.01.031

Krittanawong, C. (2019). The promises of machine learning in the era of big data. JACC: Basic to Translational Science, 4(3), 413-413. doi: 10.1016/j.jacbts.2019.04.002

Obermeyer, Z., & Emanuel, E. J. (2016). Predicting the future - Big data, machine learning, and clinical medicine. New England Journal of Medicine, 375(13), 1216-1219. doi: 10.1056/NEJMp1606181

Rajkomar, A., Dean, J., & Kohane, I. (2019). Machine learning in medicine. New England Journal of Medicine, 380(14), 1347-1358. doi: 10.1056/NEJMra1814259

Wang, L., & Wong, A. (2020). Advancements and frontiers in artificial intelligence and its application in medicine. Journal of Healthcare Engineering, 2020, 1-2. doi: 10.1155/2020/8878407

World Health Organization. (2016). Global strategy on human resources for health: Workforce 2030. Retrieved from https://www.who.int/hrh/resources/globstrathrh-2030/en/

www.ingramcontent.com/pod-product-compliance
Lightning Source LLC
LaVergne TN
LVHW012121070526
838202LV00056B/5816